WHAT ARE WORKERS' RIGHTS?

By Jennifer Lombardo

Published in 2025 by
KidHaven Publishing, an Imprint of Greenhaven Publishing, LLC
2544 Clinton Street
Buffalo, NY 14224

Designer: Deanna Lepovich
Editor: Jennifer Lombardo

Photo credits: Cover (top) Supavadee butradee/Shutterstock.com; cover (bottom) F Armstrong Photography/Shutterstock.com; p. 5 (top) nimito/Shutterstock.com; p. 5 (bottom) fizkes/Shutterstock.com; p. 7 Dietmar Temps/Shutterstock.com; p. 9 rob zs/Shutterstock.com; p. 11 Everett Collection/Shutterstock.com; p. 13 Science History Images/Alamy Stock Photo; p. 15 Cory Seamer/Shutterstock.com; p. 17 Ringo Chiu/Shutterstock.com; p. 19 MT-R/Shutterstock.com; p. 21 white snow/Shutterstock.com.

Library of Congress Cataloging-in-Publication Data

Names: Lombardo, Jennifer, author.
Title: What are workers' rights? / Jennifer Lombardo.
Description: Buffalo : KidHaven Publishing, 2025. | Series: What's the issue? | Includes index.
Identifiers: LCCN 2023049936 | ISBN 9781534547865 (library binding) | ISBN 9781534547858 (paperback) | ISBN 9781534547872 (ebook)
Subjects: LCSH: Employee rights–Juvenile literature. | Labor laws and legislation–Juvenile literature. | COVID-19 (Disease)–Law and legislation–Juvenile literature. | Industrial safety–Law and legislation–Juvenile literature. | Industrial hygiene–Law and legislation–Juvenile literature.
Classification: LCC K1705 .L66 2025 | DDC 331.01/1–dc23/eng/20231024
LC record available at https://lccn.loc.gov/2023049936

Printed in the United States of America

Some of the images in this book illustrate individuals who are models. The depictions do not imply actual situations or events.

CPSIA compliance information: Batch #CSKH25: For further information contact Greenhaven Publishing LLC at 1-844-317-7404.

Please visit our website, www.greenhavenpublishing.com. For a free color catalog of all our high-quality books, call toll free 1-844-317-7404 or fax 1-844-317-7405.

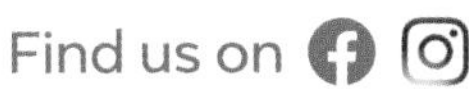

CONTENTS

Rights for All

No matter what job a person does, all workers **deserve** certain rights. A right is something a person should have just because they're a person. It's important for businesses to treat workers with fairness and respect. However, workers haven't always had the rights they have today.

In general, employers, or businesses, want to make as much money as possible. The more time employees, or workers, work each day and the less they're paid, the more money their employer makes. Employees have been fighting against unfair treatment since before the United States was a country.

Facing the Facts

About 10 percent of American workers are self-employed, or work for themselves.

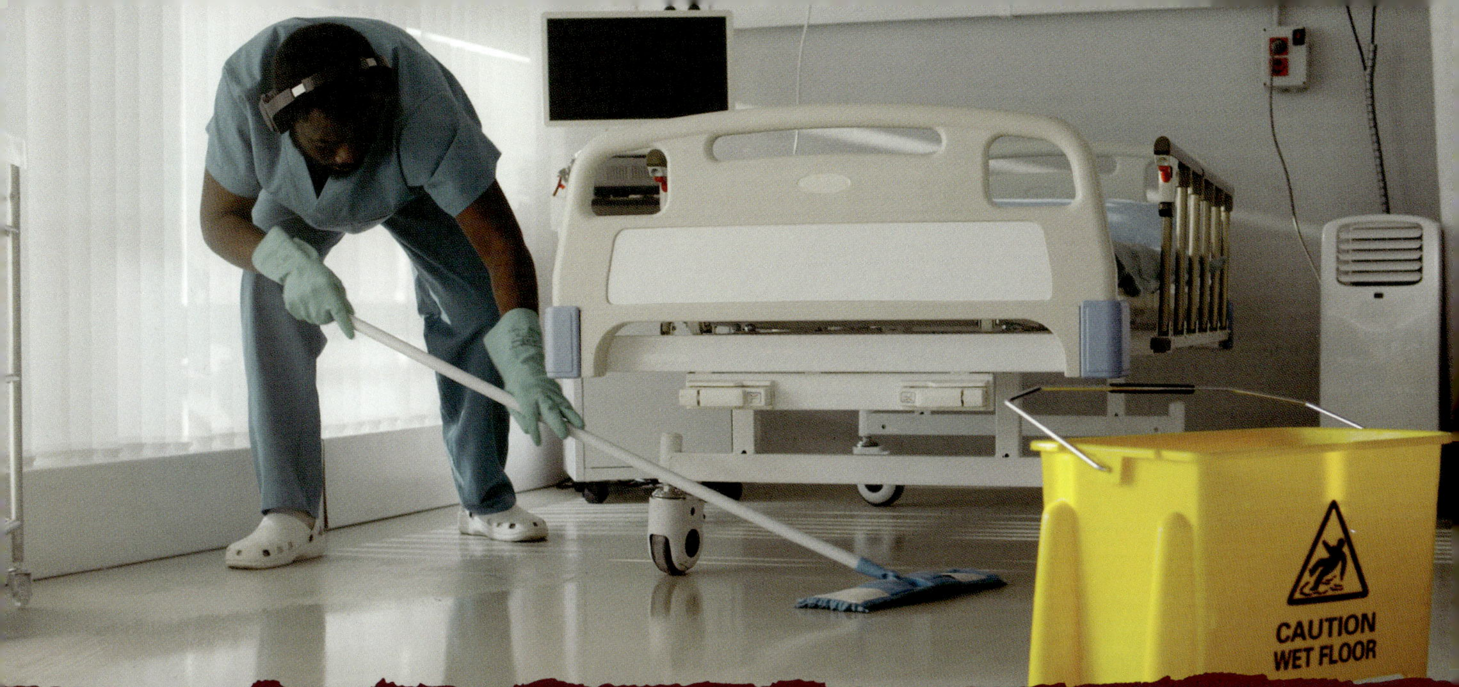

No matter what job a person does, they deserve to be treated fairly and respectfully.

Health and Safety

In the 1800s, many people worked in factories. The working conditions were unhealthy and unsafe. Employees worked up to 16 hours per day. They breathed in the smoke and dust the machines gave off. This gave many people health problems. The machines were also dangerous, or unsafe, in other ways, and many people were hurt or killed in work accidents.

At this time, low pay meant families often sent their children to work to help bring in more money for their family. Many kids started to work when they were around eight years old. They were paid very little, and their work was often dangerous.

Facing the Facts

A **strike** is one of the main tools that workers can use to fight against unfair treatment. The first strike in the United States happened in 1786. Printers in Philadelphia, Pennsylvania, went on strike until they were paid more for their work.

In some parts of the world, children still need to get jobs to help their family. In the United States, some states are lowering the legal, or lawful, working age so employers can hire kids as young as 14 for dangerous, low-paying jobs.

Uniting for a Cause

Child labor and dangerous working conditions were two big reasons why workers started creating unions. On their own, a person who asked for changes couldn't do much. When workers started banding together, they had much more power. They could strike, **picket**, and **boycott** to hurt employers.

The work of unions gave many workers a number of the rights they have today, such as an eight-hour workday and at least one day off per week. Because unions worked so well, employers didn't like them. Even today, some employers try to stop employees from unionizing. This is called union-busting, and it's often against the law.

Facing the Facts

Sometimes employers hire new people to replace their striking workers so the striking workers have less power to get employers to make changes. These new employees are sometimes called "scabs."

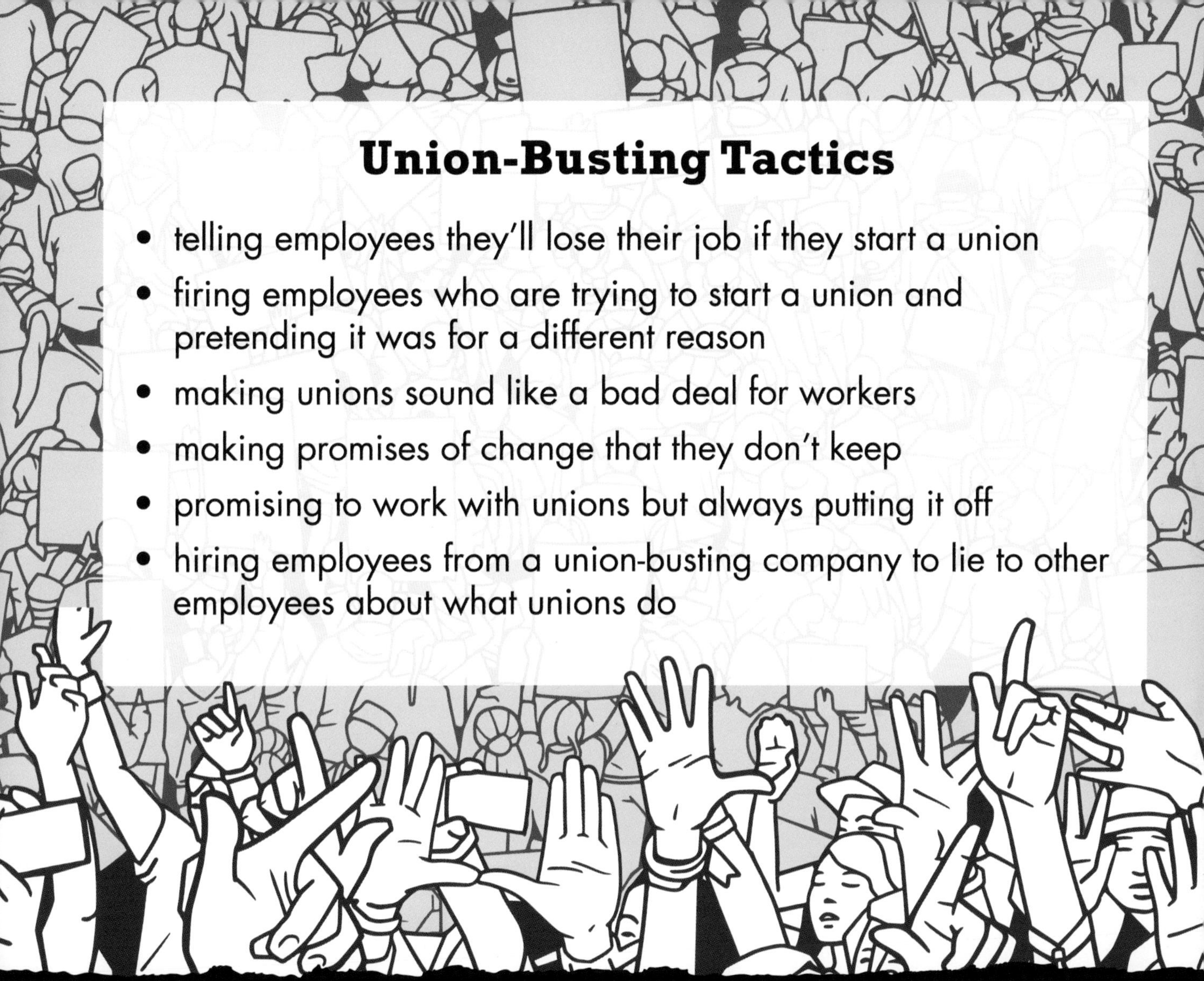

Union-Busting Tactics

- telling employees they'll lose their job if they start a union
- firing employees who are trying to start a union and pretending it was for a different reason
- making unions sound like a bad deal for workers
- making promises of change that they don't keep
- promising to work with unions but always putting it off
- hiring employees from a union-busting company to lie to other employees about what unions do

This list gives some of the tactics, or actions, employers use to try to stop employees from forming unions in their workplace.

A Sad Event

For a long time, any changes unions made only applied to some workers. **Activists** who tried to get workers' rights laws passed for all workplaces often failed. Then, in 1911, the Triangle Shirtwaist Factory in New York City caught fire. The factory doors were kept locked to stop employees from leaving to take breaks, so when the fire started, many workers couldn't get out. In the end, 146 people died.

The fire made many people start paying more attention to workers' rights. Today, laws say workplaces need to keep fire doors unlocked, have more than one exit, and have working smoke alarms.

Facing the Facts

Between 1906 and 1946, states started passing workers' compensation laws. These laws say that employers must pay for the medical bills of any employee who gets hurt at work through no fault of their own.

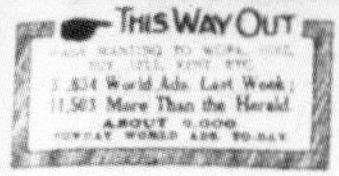

The World.
"Circulation Books Open to All."
NEW YORK, SUNDAY, MARCH 26, 1911
PRICE FIVE CENTS

154 KILLED IN SKYSCRAPER FACTORY FIRE; SCORES BURN, OTHERS LEAP TO DEATH.

TAGGING VICTIMS FOR IDENTIFICATION.

700 WORKERS, MOSTLY GIRLS, TRAPPED; BODIES OF DEAD HEAP THE STREETS; ONLY ONE FIRE ESCAPE FOR ALL.

Employees Caught on Eighth, Ninth and Tenth Floors—The Blaze Spreads with Great Rapidity—Victims Jump from Window Ledges with Clothing Aflame and Pile Up Below, Dead and Dying—Life Nets Either Torn from Grasp of Rescuers or Burst by Force of Numbers—Criminal Negligence May Be Charged for Locked Fireproof Doors Leading to Stairs—Blaze Is in Triangle Waist Co. Rooms, Washington Place and Greene St.

At 4.35 o'clock yesterday afternoon fire springing from a source that may never be positively identified was discovered in the rear of the eighth floor of the ten-story building at the northwest corner of Washington place and Greene street, the first of three floors occupied as a factory of the Triangle Waist Company.

At 11.30 o'clock Chief Croker made this statement:

"Every body has been removed. The number taken out, which includes those who jumped from the windows, is 141. The number of those that have died so far in the hospitals is seven, which makes the total number of deaths at this time 148."

At 2 o'clock this morning Chief Croker estimated the total dead as one hundred and fifty-four. He said further: "I expected something of this kind to happen in these so-called fire-proof buildings, which are without adequate protection as far as fire-escapes are concerned."

More than a third of those who lost their lives did so

...

the dreadful toll may be traced. Two other elevators were there, but were not in operation.

The property damage resulting from the fire did not exceed $100,000.

To accommodate the unprecedented number of bodies, the Charities pier at the foot of East Twenty-sixth street was opened, for the first time since the Slocum disaster, with which this will rank, for no fire in a building in New York ever claimed so many lives before.

Inspection by Acting Superintendent of Buildings Ludwig will be made the basis for charges of criminal negligence on the ground that the fire-proof doors leading to one of the inclosed tower stairways were locked.

The list of dead and injured will be found on page 4.

Streets Littered with Bodies of Men and Women.

...

first signs that persons in the street knew that these three top stories had turned into red furnaces in which human creatures were being caught and incinerated was when screaming men and women and boys and girls crowded out on the many window ledges and threw themselves into the streets far below.

They jumped with their clothing ablaze. The hair of some of the girls streamed up of flame as they leaped. Thud after thud sounded on the pavements. It is the ghastly fact that on both the Greene street and the Washington place sides of the building there grew mounds of the dead and

...

drifted away bodies burned to bare bones. There were skeletons bending over sewing machines.

Heroic Elevator Boys Saved Hundreds.

The elevator boys saved hundreds. They each made twenty trips from the time of the alarm until twenty minutes later when they could do no more. Fire was streaming into the shaft, flames biting at the cables. They fled for their own lives.

This front-page news article from 1911 reported on the Triangle Shirtwaist Factory fire. The death count was later corrected.

New Laws

The 1930s was a time of social reform, or change, in the United States. Some laws that were passed at that time were the National Labor Relations Act (NLRA), the Social Security Act, and the Fair Labor Standards Act.

The NLRA gave workers the right to unionize without being **retaliated** against by their employers. Part of the Social Security Act said people who lose their job through no fault of their own can be paid what's called unemployment insurance while they look for another job. The Fair Labor Standards Act limited the workweek to 40 hours.

Facing the Facts

Even though it's not legal for employers to retaliate against workers, some do. Retaliation can look like being fired for a made-up reason, being given more work than everyone else, or being given the worst jobs to do.

When people say someone is "collecting unemployment," they mean unemployment insurance payments. During the **Great Depression**, men such as these had to go to their local unemployment office to get their check each week. Today, people can use the internet to apply for their check.

Loopholes

Today, there are many laws that protect workers' rights. However, sometimes there are loopholes, or ways businesses can get around those laws. For example, many laws don't cover people who take gigs. These are jobs where workers can set their own hours, but the pay is often very low.

If a gig is a person's only job, they might need to work up to 100 hours per week to make enough money to buy what they need. The business they work for doesn't have to pay them **minimum wage** for their work. It also doesn't need to pay them overtime, or extra money for each hour over 40 they work in a week.

Facing the Facts

Extra things employers give employees are called benefits. They include paid time off and health insurance, which helps cover the cost of medical bills. Many workers are fighting for better benefits.

Driving for Uber or Lyft is a gig.
This picture from 2019 shows striking Uber
and Lyft drivers picketing for better working conditions,
including better pay.

Still Fighting

Workers are still fighting to get the rights they deserve. Many strike for better pay. Instead of a minimum wage, workers today want a living wage, or enough money to live on. This amount varies, or changes, from place to place.

Many workers also want better working conditions. These can include more time off, more breaks, better workplace safety, and more respect from their employers. Studies have shown that happier workers do better work, so better working conditions are good for employees, employers, and customers or patients.

Facing the Facts

Women and people of color are often paid less than white men, so many workers are also fighting to be paid the same amount as their coworkers for doing the same work.

In 2023, Hollywood writers and actors went on strike for more than 100 days. They wanted better pay as well as a promise that employers would not use **artificial intelligence** (AI) to take away their jobs.

COVID-19 Changes Things

When the sickness known as COVID-19 spread around the world, millions of people were let go from their jobs and had to collect unemployment. Many governments paid those people extra money for a while because the workers couldn't look for other jobs at the time.

People working during this time found out that, in some cases, they were being paid less than people who were unemployed. Anger about low pay pushed workers to fight harder for their rights. They quit bad jobs and would only take better ones. Many employers had to start offering better pay and benefits to get workers.

Employees whose jobs are done mostly on a computer can often do their work at home. After the COVID-19 lockdowns ended, many people fought for the right to keep working from home.

Facing the Facts

Some employers didn't give their employees the right tools to keep themselves and others safe from COVID-19. This was because those employers didn't want to spend money on those tools. Workers had to fight for new workplace safety measures.

Ways to Help

Even people who don't have a job can help fight for workers' rights. You can do this by showing solidarity with workers. This means standing up for them and listening when they talk about the problems they're trying to solve, or fix, in their workplaces.

Workers fighting for their rights might picket outside a store or call for a boycott of a business. If you see an actual picket line, you can choose not to cross it. If workers call for a boycott, you can choose not to buy anything from that business. Workers have more power when everyone stands together.

Facing the Facts

A strike is more likely to succeed when the public shows their support for it.

WHAT CAN YOU DO?

Talk to trusted adults about what rights they do or don't have at their job.

If workers call for a boycott, ask a parent or guardian if you can follow that boycott.

Learn all about your rights so you know how to fight for them when you get a job.

Support striking workers.

Write to government leaders to ask them to pass laws that give workers more rights.

Learn more about what being in a union means and what unions do for workers.

Giving workers their rights makes the world a better place for everyone, including future workers.

GLOSSARY

activist: Someone who acts strongly in support of or against an issue.

artificial intelligence: The power of a machine to imitate intelligent human behavior.

boycott: To join with others in refusing to deal with a person, organization, or country, usually to express disapproval or to force acceptance of terms.

deserve: To be worthy of.

Great Depression: A period of worldwide economic hardship and unemployment that lasted from 1929 to around 1940.

minimum wage: The lowest amount of money an employee can be paid for each hour they work.

picket: To form a line, usually holding signs, as a show of dissatisfaction with something or someone.

retaliate: To do something unkind or unfair to get even with someone.

strike: A stopping of work by employees as a protest against an employer, or taking that action.

FOR MORE INFORMATION

WEBSITES

BrainPOP: Labor Day

www.brainpop.com/socialstudies/ushistory/laborday/

Do you know why we celebrate Labor Day? Learn all about it with Tim and Moby.

Ducksters: Labor Unions

www.ducksters.com/history/us_1800s/labor_unions_industrial_revolution.php

Learn more about how unions were formed and what they did for workers.

BOOKS

Brereton, Catherine. *Working Toward Achieving Workers' Rights.* St. Catharines, Ontario: Crabtree Publishing Company, 2021.

Gilbert, Julie. *The Triangle Shirtwaist Factory Fire and the Fight for Workers' Rights.* North Mankato, MN: Capstone Press, 2021.

Hasak-Lowy, Todd. *We Are Power: How Nonviolent Activism Changes the World.* New York, NY: Abrams Books for Young Readers, 2020.

INDEX